HURRICANES

T0307588

HURRICANES

Jerome Gold, editor

Black Heron Press, Seattle
Post Office Box 95676
Seattle WA 98145

Copyright © 1994 by Jerome Gold. All rights reserved.

"After the Hurricane" originally appeared in the anthology *The Truth About the Territory*. Grateful acknowledgment is made to Owl Creek Press for permission to reprint it, and to the *Samoa News* for providing the photographs used in this book. The photograph of boats on the reef at Leloaloa Village is by Lave Tuiletufuga. The photograph of Hurricane Val beating the trees is by Monica Miller. "Preparing for the Hurricane" was originally published in The Chariton Review. Grateful acknowledgment is made to the author for permission to reprint it.

ISBN: 0-930773-35-7 (Cloth)
ISBN: 0-930773-25-X (Paper)

Black Heron Press / Post Office Box 95676 / Seattle, Washington 98145

PREPARING FOR THE HURRICANE

Behind locked shutters we squat
like cave-age folk, white eyes rolling,
with our stack of books, candles,
canned food, new plastic trashcan
filled with water.

Squirrels that each morning and afternoon
climb the banana tree in our back yard
and clutter the patio with shreds
of leaves and dark red bloom, now cling,
confused, beneath the eaves.

Wind, after all, is a kind of speech,
and when it comes, even these
taped windows will chatter. And so
we crouch here remembering water,
our pure idea of it, all our pure ideas.

—James Sallis

CONTENTS

Samoa 1989

Jerome Gold

This book is a collection of considerations about hurricanes by four writers. Two of the selections—Donna Tiapula's and John Enright's—were written during the hurricanes they describe. Three of us—Donna, John and I—write about hurricanes in Samoa. The fourth writer—Marilyn Stablein—considers some of the aftermath of the Galveston hurricane of 1983. Apart from the pleasure that reading her gives, Marilyn's essay is included here to enlarge the Samoan experience, to make of it something bigger than that lived in the archipelago alone. What this book is really about is love and grief and fear and human persistence in the face of disaster. And, in large part, it's about place.

I lived in American Samoa for part of 1982 and most of 1983. From September to September I conducted field research that would be the basis of my doctoral dissertation. Originally my intent was to get my work done and then leave. But after nine or ten months, when I had accumulated enough material for my thesis and so could leave at any time, I found myself lingering, reluctant to leave people into whose lives I had woven my own. Soon enough, however, I did leave.

While in Samoa I had collected shells. I dived a couple of times a month and collected an assortment of corals, cowries, reef clam shells and others. I brought these, and others that I had received as gifts, home with me. They were entrancingly beautiful—their symmetry convinced me that if there was not a God, there was something like God that existed apart from ourselves—and I distributed them throughout my apartment. They depressed me terribly; they reminded me of all I had lost by returning home. Soon I packed them in boxes and then put the boxes in a closet.

What had I lost? Whatever it was, I could not articulate it; I had only the sensations of grief.

I was absent from Samoa for six years, though I corresponded with a number of people for whom I had come to care when I lived there. Each year I wrote that I would return, somehow, if not that year then the one following. Finally I wrote that I would arrive on September 24th and gave the time of my arrival. I had committed myself.

I told friends in the United States that I was going for the diving and the fishing, and this was true. But truer was my going in order to be among the people I knew. The week before my flight I had to lie down frequently in order to reduce my excitement. I was afraid I would become ill from anticipation.

On the evening of the last Sunday in September, my flight put down at Pago Pago International Airport, located on the Tafuna Plain on the island of Tutuila in American Samoa. Descending, I waited to feel the heat of the island insinuate itself into the airplane. That was how I remembered the descent seven years earlier, with the heat coming into the airplane by inches until it overwhelmed the air conditioning.

No one met me at the airport and I took a taxi to Herb and Sia's Motel in the town area, as I had seven years before. I took a room with an air conditioner. Seven years earlier I passed a night in a windowless room and the sweat ran off me in rivers as I lay naked on the bed. My blood seemed to boil with the accumulation of heat until I thought I would either explode or die of dehydration. So this time I got a room with windows and an air conditioner.

The phone at the front desk was dead and the booth at the Communications Building was taken by a young man talking to his girlfriend, so I walked to the Rainmaker, the other hotel, the official one, the one owned by the government, and used a pay phone outside the lobby.

Luana answered. Hearing her tone and cadences, the rhythms of her speech, I felt that I had been away all of a week, though people's lives may have changed dramatically. She was just back from Fiji. Chuck was in Ofu with a dive charter, but he would be back tomorrow. Bruce had moved to California with his wife and stepson eighteen months ago. But Pat was still on-island and had made the stained glass windows for a new church. Sau worked at Marine Resources and Diane was the principal at one of the elementary schools. I thought that my best bet now would be to call Diane in the morning.

I had a cup of coffee at the Fia Fia, the cafe appended to the Rainmaker. I knew the cashier but could not remember her name. I asked about Ione. Ione was in the legislature now, she said. She gave me his card. She said that he always came in around 7:30 or 8:00 in the morning for breakfast.

Walking back to Herb and Sia's, I guessed the temperature to be in the low eighties. The trade winds were blowing and the sky was clear. I was not sweating too badly.

I awoke shortly after dawn, showered, dressed and set off for the Fia Fia. Tutuila is a high island. It is the top of a mountain rising from several hundred feet below the ocean's surface. Its peaks and ridges are alluded to collectively as "the mountain." This morning, thirty minutes after first light, the sun behind heavy clouds made the mountain a dull green mottled by gray shadow. Shallowness and depth, half-light and mystery. All of it so close you could lick it.

Ione did not show up and a little before 9:00 I went to the pay phone outside and called Diane. Talking with her, I had the sensation again that I had been gone but a week. It was as though I had stepped into the middle of her life and she were pulling me along like a passenger. She told me to get hold of Sau to make arrangements to come out to their village.

There is no one on Tutuila I feel closer to than Sau. No one. He came around from behind his desk and we shook hands and then embraced. He had gained weight. He was not fishing so much now, nor spending much time on his taro plantation, but passed most of his working life in his office. He apologized for not being at the airport but a family problem had come up. Perhaps living in another person's life always seems like living in a soap opera. I listened to Sau describe the plot of what had happened and mentally I traced the cultural lines of behavior to meanings and institutions; I was still the anthropologist, still under discipline. Life may have gone on without me for six years, but what I was seeing and hearing now was the life I knew.

Sau introduced me to his colleagues as "Doctor Jerome Gold," taking obvious pride in my accomplishment, for, in large part, it was his accomplishment too. We made a plan to meet at his office at 4:00. From here we would go on to his village.

In the afternoon I returned to the cafe at the Rainmaker. At a table to the side sat a fit-looking man talking to a woman beside him. His face was expressive and he gestured with his hands. I did not know the woman.

"Ione."

I watched his face as the recognition came.

"Jerry." He stood up. "I never expected to see you again." Sau had said the same thing. It was what everybody said.

Ione and I stared at each other for a moment, he made a short, glad sound and we clasped each other's shoulders.

Sitting, we each remarked on how white the other's hair had grown. He introduced me to his friend. It was apparent they had been together for some time. When I knew him before he was married to someone else. That one was from Hawaii; this one was from Western Samoa by way of Carson, California.

We talked about a *palagi* we had known. Ione had liked him because he, Ione, could anger him at will. I regarded the man as one of the two cruelest people I had ever known.

Then Ione said: "Jerry, you are the only honest *palagi* I ever met. I don't know if you are a Christian, but...." He talked on about my honesty and about how all other *palagi* are liars and thieves. He was a poet and a *tulafale*, or orator chief, and his poetry was heavy with Christian themes and symbolism. His was the Christianity of fire and vengeance, of justice and death. I envied him greatly: it had been fifteen years since I was so certain of the rightness of my life as Ione was of his.

We decided to meet later in the week for breakfast. We embraced again. "Welcome home," Ione said.

There is only one highway on Tutuila and it traverses the island along its southern shore but not its northern shore. Feeder roads come off the highway and serve the villages on the north side. Sau's village is one of these. Driving east, we passed landmarks I knew: the house where Bruce had lived; the reef where, fishing one night, I stepped into a hole and, refusing to let go of the catch bag I carried in one hand or the light and spear I held in the other, I came perilously close to getting pulled out to sea and had to call for Bruce to rescue me; Two-dollar Beach; Uele's house; Vaouli's house and store; the longliner rusting away on the reef where it wrecked while its crew was partying (and now another one, one that was not there six years ago, could be seen sitting upright on the reef at Aunuu, as if waiting to be boarded); the church where we made our turn onto the blacktop that would take us over the island's spine and spiral us down into Sau's village and finally to his house. Kathy, Sau's and Diane's daughter, used to run the road to the top of the pass and then back down. She was sixteen then. Now, in 1989, she lived in Hawaii.

Sau and Diane both asked me what changes I saw in Samoa. Everybody I met told me they did not expect ever to see me again and asked me what changes I saw.

Diane said that when I left Samoa in 1983 she was worried about me; I looked as if I were returning to all the burdens of the world. Everybody I saw told me how much better I looked now, but also that I looked the same.

Later she said that when I was here before I was "a typical graduate student." I had no opinions; I would tell her and Sau of things I had learned but I had no opinions about these things. She said that I had not wanted to participate, only to observe. Now, she said, I had changed. I was more critical. She and Sau agreed that I was taller now.

Sau said to me one night: "I wish you would retire in Samoa. Sell your business, come to Samoa...."

In January 1987, Hurricane Tusi swept the island of Ta'u, in the Manu'a Group, clean of everything that stood more than a few inches above the ground. All housing was destroyed. Tree trunks were sheered so evenly as to have been cut with a chain saw.

Nobody on Tutuila, the main island of American Samoa, knew this was happening. On Tutuila people were readying themselves for the hurricane. Only when they realized that Tusi would not get this far west did they realize, too, that they had no radio contact with Ta'u. (Listening to Sau tell his story, I recalled suddenly the young woman I had met on Olosega who recounted her waking one morning in 1966 to the screeching of that season's hurricane ripping the metal roof off her house: "I thought it was Armageddon.")

When the hurricane passed, the government sent Sau up in a light airplane to survey the island. From the sky, neither Sau nor the pilot could see anything moving. There were no people. There was only wreckage. The airplane could not land because of the rubble cluttering the airstrip. Using a portable speaker, Sau spoke into the air below. He told the air that the hurricane had gone but the landing strip had to be cleared so that the airplane could land. He said into the air that people must clear the airstrip. One at a time, people began to come out from under the rubble. Sau told them again to clear the airstrip. Then he and the pilot returned to Tutuila to refuel.

When they were able to land at Ta'u they learned that everybody had survived the hurricane. Animals were not so fortunate. The doctor recounted seeing a pig fly past the dispensary. "I didn't know pigs could fly," he said. This line about pigs flying became a joke on Ta'u. Someone would say "I didn't know pigs could fly" and it was good for a laugh. (In fact, I heard it again in 1993 on Tutuila and it was still considered funny.)

But people were dazed. They had to be told to do the things that everyday sense should have told them to do. They had to ensure their water supply. They had to clear the wreckage. They had to replant. They had to rebuild. They needed to be told to do each of these things; on their own they seemed not to be able to follow their thoughts through to action. Two and a half years later much of Ta'u still lay ruined.

I said to Diane one evening that one of the things I most liked about Samoa was the edge of fear—of hurricanes mostly, but of the sea, too—the sense that we live in an uncontrollable universe and the perspective that knowledge gives. We can be wiped away like writing from a chalkboard and we would not have left even a thought of ourselves. Living in Seattle, it is easy to forget what fragile organisms make up our species, what luck we have had simply to have survived this long.

Some time later Sau asked me what I found in Samoa that I didn't in Seattle. I told him that life in Samoa feels more complete than in Seattle where social life revolves almost exclusively around business or work. To which Sau said "Thank you."

The last time I saw my friend John Kneubuhl I put Sau's question to him: what was the difference between life on the mainland and life in Samoa? "No affect," he said about the mainland. He said it as soon as the question was out of my mouth; it required no reflection at all.

That was it, of course. It was what I forsook when I returned to the United States in 1983. Call it love. Or place. Call it possibility. I had been edging all around it without recognizing it. And I was going to leave it again soon.

Samoa had been in drought for two months before I arrived and there had not been any significant rainfall since. Sau had the only water in the village now, having found and tapped an underground spring. He rigged a pipe outside so that other families could shower and get water for cooking. He did not have to do this: the water is on his family's land and he could have kept it for his family's use exclusively if he chose. But from another point of view, he did have to do it: he is a member of the village and expected, therefore, to be concerned for its welfare.

Toward the end of my second week in Samoa the weather began to change: clouds came and stayed, humidity increased. Half an inch of rain fell on the western part of the island. On the north side, we suddenly got wind, signaling the beginning of hurricane season.

Two days later the rain came in earnest, the wind behind it, blowing it across the mountain in bunches so that I could not see the green of the forest for the gray water. The rain enveloped the mountain like a slow-moving fish's mouth.

Hurricane Ofa 1990

Donna Tiapula

Feb. 2, 1990 is the date of Hurricane Ofa. I have decided to write a letter or report about it. Electricity is out & likely won't be back for a day or two. This isn't a terrible fact for us. It happens here frequently. We have 4 kerosene lamps and 2 Coleman pump lamps. They sit ready in the corner of the front room. We use gas for cooking. This morning I bought 8 bags of ice and packed the freezer. I then covered the inside tap with blankets, closed the lid & added another blanket. It should keep for 3 or 4 days.

The storm is supposed to hit this evening about 7 pm

It has been exciting. Jerry Gold said the hurricane added the element of danger that makes life interesting. I agree some with this. Samoan weather is dull. I teach a unit on weather in science. I always do it in Jan., otherwise the data collected bore the students. January & February have a chance for excitement. By 7 pm the hurricane should have some excitement for us.

We have followed the path of the hurricane as given by reports on the radio. We live on Tutuila. The storm is 200 miles NW of us. We will have the edge hit us since the storm is moving directly south.

This morning I packed the house. All of my school supplies went into garbage bags. I store them in boxes, so we have 20 black plastic bags in my room. All of Fia's stuff into boxes and bags. Clothes off the hangers and into drawers. Computer and TV back into their original boxes with foam packing and into black plastic bags. Cushions off the chairs and around TV & computer. Then mats tied around all of it & rewrapped in heavy plastic. All the floor mats up & on the bed. Covered with plastic & taped down.

If the storm veers east & hits us we will be OK up to 120 mph winds. Roof will be torn off & everything wet but OK. After 120 nothing stands up and we worry about life only. Three years ago Manu'a was hit by winds over 200 mph. Trees were sheered off like a giant's ax had gone through. Every man-made structure was gone & the wood & building supplies had vanished. In that type of storm a person has no protection for things. Most of our storms are 90 to 120. Tonight the report says 85. Not too bad.

I am lying on a mat. The house we live in has no real walls, just screen windows. We have canvas curtains we put up. Usually they are only tied at the top but now the sides are hooked on nails & rope is crisscrossed in front to hold them in. I have the door open so I can watch the waves. Winds aren't bad yet.

1:00 pm

The waves are getting worse. Last night some of the waves were way up near the homes and the bridge to the school was under water. The sea is hard to describe. Usually it is such a beautiful deep blue & now it is green and ugly. The sea has claimed 20 ft of land and nothing can withstand it. Several small cooking houses have been swept out.

When I first married Fia I was so disappointed we did not own a lot of seashore land. The ideal home is built on the beach with waves for company. A large picture window. That idea was dashed, since we have only 2 or 3 pieces of seashore land and those are in the middle of the village. We live about 300 ft from the sea and up on a little hill 6 or 7 ft high. We have a clear view of the sea, but we're not on the sea.

5:30 pm

Two small homes have been destroyed, gone totally today. We went down and moved furniture. The bay is filled with waves on the reef 20 to 30 ft tall. Not one or two waves, but 100's an hour. We know the storm will hit in 2 or 3 hours.

The strangest thing I have seen is bouncing waves. The waves are coming in so heavy & fast, the entire wave bounces on top of the one going out. It is impossible to describe the force of these waves. The beautiful blue sparkling bay is now a churning gray angry monster. If we could somehow tap this energy source it would be energy for months.

Can you imagine Swains Island right now? It is an atoll. Not a volcanic mountain. Just a bump of coral resting 2 or 3 ft above the sea. The highest point is 6 ft, where the church is. It has several times been hit by waves washing clear over it. Three years ago they went underwater with people tied to trees. Fia has gotten to know the people, since he has been there several times. John went there this year. We worry about how they are doing.

Saturday

10:00 am

Storm is here. It is really blowing now. No longer can I watch the waves. Wind is too fierce. We cannot see the bay, rain and wind obstructs the view. Wind is up. Noise is a problem. The strength of nature is scary. Man is a puny thing.

Radio announcement in Samoan. "Will all maintenance men please report. The high winds have damaged the solar system. We believe it will fall, if not quickly repaired." The English version explained it was the solar panels at the hospital.

Weather report. Storm is stronger than expected. Sustained winds up to 85 mph. Gusts up to 117. I can't imagine Savai'i where sustained winds are up to 114 and gusts are up to 200. I am scared here.

The waves have brought rubbish up to the *malae*. It is 80 to 100 ft from the high-tide mark. The waves were terrible last night. 6 of the seaside homes are gone. We have another high tide at 2 pm & the wind is still blowing. All seashore homes have been abandoned.

No, Jerry Gold isn't right. Hurricanes are not enjoyable. I am so thankful that this one didn't hit us. We have only the edge. The eye is 200 miles west of us. I feel sorry for Savai'i, but rejoice it is not us. No Christian feeling of wishing I could take the pain for others. I only rejoice it did not move east last night.

1:00

Worse, worse, worse. Can it get stronger? Radio says yes. I hope not. The rain & wind calmed down. Fia went out for pictures & I went to look. I shouldn't have gone. It is depressing. I couldn't see most of the destruction. All the houses seaside have been damaged. Destruction is terrible. Terrible because very likely my house will be next in the next few hours. The winds are worse.

John is sitting on the chair next to me, his chin on the table. He is so sad & worried. Ben wants to play games to take his mind off it. I am too worried & nervous to play.

12:00

We have one canvas curtain that has one gap that is not tied shut. One head can look out. If a gust hits, you get a face full of water. John started a silly joke. *'Ola* means Oh! in Samoan. Now as a person watches, *'Ola* or *'ola'ola* registers how bad it is. *Ola'ola'ola* was a 30 ft wave breaking over the top of Teo's roof or Logo's house breaking in 1/2 & floating out to sea. *'Ola* is a toilet sitting on top of a wave.

12:30

Wind is much worse. Tide is high at 2:00. The ocean is now in the *malae* 80 ft above high-tide mark. All seaside houses are gone. Rubbish is in big piles 100 ft from high tide near our home.

We now have a family of children here in Ben's room. Their home is gone. The oldest daughter is watching the four youngest who are all crying. They are all wet, cold and tired. I fed them & now they are trying to sleep.

I am so scared. My stomach aches. I am angry. Angry at Fia. It is irrational but when I get scared I want to pull into myself & be left alone. If I could read I'd be OK, but I can't. I must keep curtains secure, a continuous job. Sweeping water out. The boys must be watched & talked to, & now this family.

One good thing. Fia went down to help a family nail things down. On his way back he saw one of our roofing irons was loose. He was able to nail it back on & tie the corner down. His helping others paid off. It saved our roof for another hour or so.

Leaks are bad in kitchen, bathroom & area in back of house. Buckets of water. Not really leaks now, just massive water everywhere. The wind is blowing so hard now, the walls vibrate. The roofing irons shudder & shake. I wish time would pass faster.

1:30

More time, but not enough. Trees down everywhere around us. I made 4 pots of *saimin* & corned beef for people. I keep hoping our house makes it for 1 more hour. Should be over about 6 or 7. Hour by hour I pray for more safety. I write to help me be less nervous.

4:30

It feels like 72 hours since I started this. We have 4 families living here. One family, a wave came & took their house & everything. They climbed through a back window as the house moved. They got the baby & 2 kids out. The waves had cut them off from the village. They had to climb the mountain & come in over the plantation bridge by the pond which is 3 ft under water. Part of the church next to them crumbled into the sea like a cracker, they said. Lost everything but a baby bottle. Other 3 families have their things saved in a lean-to shelter near our house.

A frightening time. A nice thing about tornadoes is that they are over with fast. Bad damage, but this slow pain is worse than one big jerk.

6:00

I am writing this in hopes that by writing about it I will release some of the fear & tension I feel. The long day Friday and this terrible day I don't think will ever end. Not much to do now. My roof shakes & with each gust I fear the roof will go. My weak boxes I fear will not stand up to the wind & God forbid those terrible waves. Nothing to do is worse. No computer, no garden. No one feels like talking. We can't hear and we are all too scared.

I forgot one impression. When I went down at 2:00 every house was spotty. All walls & surfaces green spotty. At first it didn't register. The leaves had been torn to bits & houses & ground were covered with these leaf pieces. Amazing.

I sure hope no one turns on the electricity. The lines are down everywhere. I know people want lights & refrigeration but it should be checked first. My walls are wet all the way through. Nothing would be safe.

John & Ben are pacing the floor, caged lions. They want to go out and explore. Winds are worse. Roofing irons, branches, coconuts & wood are flying, so it is too dangerous.

7:30

I've gathered some news. Only one teacher & the janitor have a house left. All other teachers lost it all.

9:00

Thank God another family is here. Their house just went. Now we worry about how our house will hold. If it does, for how long? I thought it would be over with by 6, but now Fia says my math was wrong. It will not be over till 12 Sunday.

Page after page I write & it still goes on. Stop! I told Fia to zap it with the TV control. Turn the channel, start a new story. Shows finish their trouble in 30 or 60 minutes. I want it over. It is hard to describe. Where houses once stood—nothing. Walis, roofs & foundations gone. No evidence of existence. Boulder 3 to 4 ft high carried in by waves. Places where land is gone.

10:00

I'm still waiting for it to stop. What will these people do for food, clothing & shelter? Will my house stand? That is the main question. In no way can I claim to be a generous person. I am selfish. I think of others only after myself. I think of my kids, myself & Fia. Everyone & everything comes after that.

Water & wind. Terrible. Can't keep house dry.

Sunday morning

7:00

At 11:00 my roof was torn partly off. We had rain pouring in. We had a ceiling in that area so we didn't see sky immediately, but soon the ceiling collapsed.

We carried all the boxes out of that area & started sweeping water out. We swept it into the cracks in the cement floor. Our home is not a standard American home.

What a terrible sound. The screech of the nails pulling out, & the loudness of it. Knowing we no longer had protection from that monster of a storm. I can't describe my feelings. To be watching the destruction is one thing, but to be a part of it—news reporters must feel like that. No matter how bad it is, they can always hop a plane & write a report in an air-conditioned home. It is different when it is happening to you.

Yet I feel ashamed. I lost 1/4 of my roof & we have water in our house, but we were lucky.

Last night after the major move & clean-up the teenagers set up a mat in a dry corner & played cards for a bag of penny candy I had bought for my class. No one slept. The noise, the wet, the fear.

My main concern was survival. If the storm had gotten worse, where would we go? I packed a plastic bag full of sheets, clothes & a few books and set it by the back door in case we had to evacuate. Fia felt it was too dangerous to be out in the dark. He made a safe corner in one room. He took good care of us. I am ready to nominate him for sainthood today. While others were talking & socializing Friday, he got things ready. He takes care of us. No luxury, just basic care. He speaks of his love through his actions. That is love stronger than the mere words "I love you" or flowers or candy.

Sunday

8:30 am

My oven is filled with 3 boxes of chicken & 5 lbs of sausage. I will feed my little families. Everyone is up & out. Fia & boys are trying to mend roof. Picking up rubbish & nailing houses together.

2:00pm

Storm is over. No sunshine, but rain, and wind is down

to 40 & 50. Gone. Gone is the very land where houses once stood. All electrical lines down. The mountain & land are stripped of all green leaves. I get dizzy outside since trees & buildings are all slanting.

4 pm

I went over to the school. Bridge is gone. Waves washed through, taking desks, walls, cupboards & all out. Bathroom is gone. Waves just went over the 7 ft sea wall.

Buildings being gone is not as disturbing to my mind as the place they were on being gone. No bridge, I can accept, but the land on each side where the bridge was is gone. Graves are on the top of the land now since all land around them was washed away. I teach geological concepts of slow change, but a new riverbed in one night! I no longer live in Aoa, or at least the Aoa I knew. Think of opening your door one morning & finding new roads & streets & buildings. A new town. Maybe it is OK but it isn't the one you expect to see. I keep shaking my head to adjust my eyesight.

Announcement just now—no school. The island is at a standstill. Lines are down, no communication out or in. Roads blocked.

Monday afternoon

Fia went to work. I've been to the school. No supplies left. I have one room left. We put all the chairs & desks in there & locked them up. The rest of the place is worthless.

I came home & tried to get some order. 2 families moved out to their homes. Another family is over looking at their place.

Fia came home & said he dived into the ocean for his roof. He came home with nails & material for our home. Wind is still blowing, but not like last night.

Tuesday afternoon

I went to town. Radio called a principals' meeting, but governor arrived so our meeting was canceled. No electricity for a long time. 5 schools plus mine wiped out. Other schools damaged. Computers down. Roofs off most government offices. Damage everywhere. Radio carries only news.

Wednesday

I worked at school all morning. Not much to do since damage is everywhere. Government still trying to estimate damage. Found out Swains was wiped out. They will fly an air drop of food & emergency stuff tomorrow. No news from Western Samoa.

Thursday

Principals' meeting. 6 schools will be closed & moved to other schools. Mine is one of these. We have no material, chairs. We come into the school as beggars. School is off for 2 weeks. 5 buses damaged. Damage is everywhere. Most north shore damage is from waves. One village, Onenoa, is gone. 1 house left. Destruction everywhere. Rubbish & more rubbish. My ice is still holding. I cooked fish for five families last night. Chicken tonight. Trying to use up all of it before it spoils.

News from Western Samoa still not clear or complete. Damage much worse than ours. 7 known dead, but that isn't final since no one has been to outlying villages or Savai'i, a major island. No dead in American Samoa. We are lucky.

Friday

We are now a disaster area. President gave permission. We need the aid. I don't know how it will work. Insurance covers the government damage but no one else has insurance. We don't. If our home is gone, it is just gone. We were so lucky that we lost so little. Fia and I lost just the corner. The big guest house suffered wind damage & Mamea's house suffered some rain & wind damage. It cost just $400 to fix our roof & wires. We lost the pigs' roof & one pig got hurt. Hope he lives. Only a little wind damage to trees.

Saturday

In the village of Alao, a village right on the sea, one man caught parrot fish and a mullet up on the *malae* near his house during the waves.

Bulldozers came out & cleared a path through our village so cars can now come in & out. We had to walk over the hill all week to get out. No electricity for 2 months at least. Clean-up will take a long time. Bulldozers will be here for a week to carry off all the rubbish & dead trees.

The last family moved out of our house today. Thank God. We ate the last food tonight & had champagne to celebrate. Some left from New Year's. Now we have much to celebrate. I am so happy it is over.

Sunday

Started to unpack stuff. Put up pictures on the walls. Put the books back. Front room empty & back in place. All the chairs had been piled up in the back of the front room. Now mats on the floor & no people here. One night we slept person-to-person in long lines in the two safe rooms. Now I have a bed. Boys have a bedroom. I love it. I am sitting in the rocking chair with my feet up in the window. The sea is again so beautiful.

I spent one day cutting the bushes down & raking the front yard. We have raked & cleaned the back yard & the side by the guest house. We only have to clean the clothes-line yard, basketball yard, pigpen yard, garden-&-pond yard & the avocado yard. By the time we get all the yards cleaned & trees cut & dragged off it will be a month & the electricity will be back on.

We are all OK & that is the main thing. We didn't lose much. Of course my store of food & extras, but nothing really important. I lost more in the classroom than here at home. I filed a claim of $500 worth of teaching material that was in the classroom (electric pencil sharpener, battery clock, several other small things). Most important, we are OK. Even Fia's extended family is OK. In the extended family we lost 1 house in Lauli'i & 1 built for me when we married & 1 belonging to Faioga, Fia's brother, at another village. Damage to the guest house, Mamea's house, Sina's (Fia's sister) and Imo's (Fia's brother). All minor. No real terrible place except Faioga's house. Faioga's son also got hit with roofing iron & had to be hospitalized 1 or 2 days.

Radio just now said death count in Western Samoa up to 17.

No water in our village except ours again. Water pipes got washed out. Destruction to crops bad. Breadfruit is terrible. No breadfruit till next Jan. Branches all down. No bananas for 6 months. It will be a lot of rice.

We think of you all.

Donna

Hurricane Val 1991

John Enright

6 Dec. '91
Atauloma

Bradpoet—

What do you know? The power is back on. It was off when I got home at dusk and I got all my hurricane and Coleman lanterns fired up. There's a hurricane warning for tonight, and I really didn't figure that (the power just went off again) the power would come back on. Well, I was partly right, temporarily wrong. Back to writing by hurricane lantern (that long shadow the pen makes across the page). The computer is unplugged.

Hurricane Val. Val? Sounds more like someone who wants to put fresh-ground black pepper on your salad than a storm that's going to toss your coconuts.

I left Liam in Leloaloa, where he should be safer than here. Also, I'm on medication—for one of those famous unnamed island staph infections—and considerably less than 100%.

Power back on, if flickering. Good. I foolishly took out a steak to defrost when the power came back on the first time, figuring I'd try for one more non-kerosene-cooked meal before the power went away for days.

I'm fairly prepared for the storm; although old Atauloma

has not been repaired since Hurricane Ofa 22 months ago and is less prepared than I. (She has windows that won't close for rotted jambs and rusted hinges, delaminated doors nailed shut, holes in her roof.)

Thus far the workup has been nothing like huge Ofa, but then Tusi before it was also compact and wiped Manu'a with a direct hit. Nothing to do but sit and eat steak and wait. I have a storm's supply of Old Crow, Steinlager, and Camels in the house.

Received and enjoyed your "Love Hotel: Los Angeles." Time is short; maybe we should both go for the weird more often. All these many years we've been rasping and honing these poetic skills of public exclamation in practiced politeness while voices from Blue Cheer to 2-Live Crew have grossed themselves into public consciousness.

—Saturday morning, 7 December—

Tora tora tora, baby.

Remember those word problems from grammar school math—if a train leaves Chicago, going 45 mph...? At 1 pm yesterday our waitron Val was 220 miles NW of Tutuila, traveling SE at 10 mph. At 5 am today it was 110 miles NW of Tutuila, traveling SE at the same 10 mph. Go figure.

10:30 am and it is picking up a bit. The bamboo in the

courtyard is having a go at the gutters. I have buckets positioned under all the major leaks. The latest prediction is that Val honey will pass directly over Tutuila sometime late this afternoon. The power has been permanently out since sometime during the night. Water is now gone too. Thinking of you driving out from Mapusaga on the Saturday of Ofa's approach to sit on the front veranda and watch the ocean. The surf is nowhere near as huge and confused as it was by Ofa, at least not on this shore, thus far. Of course, the longer the storm dawdles on its way here, the meaner it gets. Again, it is the waiting. The smell of kerosene in the closed-up house, funny details—the ants that have invaded my kitchen since the start of the rainy season have all disappeared since the barometer plunged. A neighbor's dog has dug herself a regular doggy fallout shelter into the face of the hill above the parking lot.

If the old roof stays on we'll be fine; if not, we're fucked.

—Noon—

An eerie calm. The latest word is the worst should begin in an hour or two. Sustained winds of 100 mph with gusts up to 140, but right this minute not a leaf is stirring. I miss Liam.

It's a couple of hours later now and, of course, nothing has happened. The barometer stays the same. It is deathly still again. It's a feeling like being stalked. Maybe the storm just went away. Called up the weather bureau again—the storm is still headed our way, but has stalled over Savai'i. Now it is expected tonight with winds gusting to 150 mph. Should I start stuffing files and books into garbage bags? Of course, when it quits Savai'i, it could head more south than east, and, being a condensed storm, spare us the worst. I am sorry for Savai'i though—once again taking the brunt of it.

—Midnight Saturday—

Just back from watching two segments of "I, Claudius" down at Tom & Nancy's. Tom and I have been talking our way through eight segments thus far. The power and water are back on; Val headed south after trashing Savai'i. The wind is still gale force and squalls still pass through with that cleansing intensity you remember, but this storm, it seems (I hope), has passed south. (As if answering me, the wind suddenly screams again through the bush, bending everything sideways in the dark, whacking the roof with its fists.) My floors are slippery with rain even though the house is as closed as I can make it. My outdoor cat is indoors.

I love this anticlimax and I miss my son asleep inside my now safe house. Thanks for talking me through the storm. I think after Ofa I became a bit storm-shy (the lights flicker), which is why I left Liam in Leloaloa in the shelter of that drastic ridge's wind shadow.

There is a drier feeling in the gusts; the barometer has crept a hair higher.

Now, as the storm withdraws, there is a certain majesty in the roar of the wind through the jungle of the ridge. In the thickest of it today before dusk, I had a bar-b-que picnic for Tom & Nancy and Richard & Dawn and their kids on my lee veranda—the one facing the southern sea. As the world howled past us we ate steak and weiners and salad and quiche and listened to Bob Dylan tapes. 'Tis passing strange. Lost napkins disappeared forever. We were ravenous. The bar-b-que blazed in the lean-on-me breeze. We talked politics. We hadn't yet heard where the storm was heading. It was a fine meal. I think folks are best in times of shared adversity.

It's late. At first light I'll thread my way through the damage between here and town to fetch Liam. We'll stop at the airport for a "burgercheese," then check in on our friends and lovers on the way home. Survival is nice, it's what life's all about; it is good to feel it like hair raising along the skin. It would feel better, I guess, to share it with someone.

It rains again, one of those wash-outs when even screams are the same as silence.

Yours,
John

7 December 1991
Atauloma

Carole—

Hurricane Val is a hundred miles away, stalled over poor Savai'i, with winds up to 150 mph. Here on its edge, and probable future course, it is intermittently violent—paroxysms of climatic anger—cyclonic arms sweeping over us.

I have stashed Liam with Sinavaiana in Leloaloa, where he should be safer, if not better entertained. Power and water are off. Another angry shiver of squall passes through.

I hope it heads more southerly than easterly when it leaves Savai'i. I don't think parts of this old, unrepaired place could take much battering by 150 mph winds. I've made all the usual preparations, and now there is little to do but wait—originally Val baby was to have hit here last night. To entertain myself I've been writing "The Ballad of Billy Smith" about the Florida rape trial. I enjoy cheap doggerel sometimes, especially when I need distraction. I miss Liam's company.

I'm sitting out on the front veranda between white-out showers. Coconuts are air-borne, but the ocean is not exceptionally wild—nothing like it was before Ofa. But then Ofa was one of the largest tropical storms ever measured. This one is more your average size, but a direct hit could easily bring back the great healing goddess FEMA. How considerate of Ms. Nature that the last three hurricanes—Tusi, Ofa, now Val—have arrived on weekends.

—Later, 5 pm—

An early dusk. I have an insane urge to go bowling. The squalls intensify, the bamboom (as Liam calls it) attacks the gutters and iron roof. It is low and lonesome here alone. The night will probably be a long one. I will try to cook some food now on the kerosene stove and the bar-b-que in the lee of the porch.

—8 pm—

I made dinner and had Richard & Dawn and Tom & Nancy over with their kids. After one very intense squall, the weather backed off and we heard on the radio that the storm had followed my wishes and turned south after trashing Savai'i. It will be blowing on this shore now but moving off, so I think we are out of it. Tomorrow I'll go and fetch Liam. Our roof is still on and my books safe.

Everyone's gone now and the wind's hit a trough. It's so quiet, the power comes back on, blinking. This should be the end of the hurricane Val report.

Sunday, Dec. 8, 2 pm

Bradpoet—

Ha! the joke was on me and my optimism. When I retired last night we had power and the prospect of the storm heading south. When I awoke there was no power and the gales had intensified. It seems Val decided to dawdle again, 50 miles south of Savai'i, and then crawl eastward. It's been another day of waiting as the storm slowly gets worse. The barometer just took another dive.

I left this morning to get Liam and made it as far as the Taputimu turnoff before being stopped by a wall of hurricane. I turned back. Now it seems it will drag by to the south of us, perhaps as close as 50 miles. The ocean is finally beginning to look like a cyclone sea.

I am getting tired of this.

Ataulama Sunday 12/8/91/1400 hrs.

barometer: 28 1/2 in.
9.65 millibars, dropping.
temp: 80 degrees F.
rel. hum.: 78%
winds gusting at 80 knots

Dear Mom,

Day two of Hurricane Val. For a day it stalled over the island of Savai'i a hundred some miles west of us. Today it is slowly crawling toward us to the south. The worst is yet to come; the barometer keeps dropping and the gusts get stronger.

It is suddenly very still. The birds and the fruitbats who have sought shelter in our narrow ocean-facing valley are busy switching roosts. And then, in the time it took to write that sentence, a 40-knot gust moved through. The sound of the wind rushing through the jungle and of the surf pounding on the reef is the soundtrack of my life.

No power. No point in listening to the outdated updates on the emergency radio channel. I can tell well enough what is important from the barometer and the face of the ocean.

A bad sign—a flight of frigate birds just arrived in the cove. They are open-ocean birds, moving ahead of the storm, looking for relative shelter.

It's the lonely waiting that gets to you. You do all you

can and then just wait, hoping the old sheet-iron roof will stay on. I miss the boy's company, though he should be safer where he is.

—Later, 1800 hours—

The storm's big winds are still coming from the north-west, behind us, sort of, as the house faces south toward the ocean, its back up against a ridge. So my seaward veranda is in the lee of the building and in this wind is, actually, surprisingly calm, in spite of the storm whizzing by on both sides and the tumbled ocean out front.

The storm has cranked up another few notches; the barometer's dropped another few millibars. Sometime tonight the wind will shift to the south and come straight on-shore. I just hope the storm's center keeps drifing south. This is a very old building.

Monday, Dec. 9, 0700 hours

Bradpoet—

By dawn's early light we are taking a trashing. The roof where I was afraid it would go—where the pillars were cracked during Ofa—went and is now in the bush up the ridge behind Susan's. That's the porch and front roof of Richard & Dawn's and Barry's apartments. The roofing irons above my dining room are peeled back and flapping. The cupola from the peak of my room is now sitting upside down in the front yard. Two of my porch doors are gone. The living room and dining room are soaked. At least the roof had the decency to break apart and not leave en masse. A lot of big coconut and breadfruit trees are down in the yard.

The wind and rain have died down, so I guess the worst passed in the night, although the weather report on the radio is seven hours old, so I'm not sure where the storm is now. Power, water, and phones are out. I can only hope Leloaloa didn't get it as badly as we did—though the direction the storm came at us, from the south—doesn't bode well for them. A lot of wet books, and roofing irons still flapping. It was a long, loud night.

I just checked my barometer. It has bottomed out. We're not out of this yet.

—12/9, 1100 hours—

The storm from hell.

The latest prediction is that Val,vastly obese by now after lingering for a long *to'onai* of overheated ocean and *Samoa i Sisifo* jungle, has not gone away. Its eye is *still* to the west of us.

In the four hours since I last wrote we have had some very heavy winds, lost more trees and more roof. It seems the worst is not past, but is yet to come. My barometer bottomed out at 28 inches, 9.48 millibars, around 0900. It is now about a quarter-inch or point 6 millibars below that; off the scale. The NOAA scenario now is for the heart of the storm to pass over us sometime this afternoon. Disaster is always imminent, always delayed.

Both Richard's and Barry's apartments are pretty much a washout, with their front roof gone. I have spent most of the time since the previous entry trying to save what I can from my dining room and living room, bagging books, stashing artwork and good mats—those not already soaked—in the laundry room. I am taking an Old Crow/ Steinlager/Camel break in my office, which I have decided is the safest room in the apartment. I've stashed all the bagged books and other valuables here. I have not yet begun bagging my poetry collection and other books in the office. I'll wait till I have to.

Everyone here—Susan is stateside, Barry and Faye (who now lives in the Makagons' old place) are in Honolulu, and Cheryl (who lives downstairs in the back) is in Apia—everyone still here (5 adults, 4 kids), save me, are moving into Faye's apartment. It's the best repaired and secure and she has a gas range. Of course, she's not here, but she'd understand. I'm going to stay up here with my books as long as possible, where I can smoke and drink and brood alone, Lear-like, on the mystical and animalistic aspects of STORM, the earth's anger.

After three days of this it is like living with an emotion. It is easiest to anthropomorphize it—an extremely upset, if not psychotically disturbed goddess. Here she is, crying her eyes out again; soon she'll start screaming and breaking things again. She wants to kill you, but she hasn't been able to focus her trauma that well thus far.

Roof irons flapping sound like a giant on the roof. I could really learn to dislike that sound.

—12/9/91, 1700 hours—

This is it, full bore from the south. I just watched the porch and roof of Susan's house disintegrate. I've bagged all the books I can—no more garbage bags. The front rooms are unvisitable, the wind and rain coming through the broken doors and windows. It strikes me that this place may very well be unlivable when this is over. I watch a roofing iron on Susan's roof waving toward my window. It doesn't do to think about Liam in Leloaloa where this incredible blow from the south is the worst-case scenario for the Bay area generally and the boats in the harbor.

The barometer, when it touched bottom, was a full half-inch off the calibrated scale—around 27.5 inches. Since the reverse blow started, it has crept a tad upward for the first time in days.

The roof irons are still peeling away from the edge of last night's damage where we lost Richard's and Barry's porch and roof. So far, the *sami*-side roof (the rusted side) has held, but we'll have another 10 hours of this, at least.

It roars and whistles like it did during Ofa, but thus far the office feels snug, even if the rest of the house is a hard-hat, hang-on-to-your-socks area.

One thing about earthquakes, they never last more than a minute, not 70-80 hours. If I wasn't so tired and half-drunk I'd be petrified. Goodby gathered objects of a lifetime. Maybe that's the simplistic point, something the Buddha said about attachments. I am not afraid for my life (the house shakes with a solid wave of angry air); that's not it. I'm not a fan of discomfort (the fingers of my left hand throb from being caught in a wind-slammed door a while ago), but there will be no denying or avoiding the discomforts of the weeks to come. But perhaps I have become too attached (Brad, you should hear how the wind whistles through this broken house!) to this house and this life and this persona (The house shakes again in a gust stronger than all before. They said it was gusting at 150 mph—it just did.) The trees will return; in fact, their wind-spread progeny will flourish. Storms make the rainforest. What makes me? These books in garbage bags? My carefully wrapped and stashed journals and manuscripts? The container of computer disks hidden in the deepest recess of my office closet?

Liam, maybe, who is not here, but afraid somewhere, without me.

—12/9/91, 2200 hours—

She howls from the south, screams actually. I was napping and was awakened by another window going in the living room. So far the office has stayed snug and dry, but it's been six hours now since the storm opened up from the south and I must wonder how long the old place can hold up to such a beating. I am so tired of listening beneath the wind for the sounds I do not want to hear. I'm a little scared by all this intensity. I couldn't leave the place now even if I wanted to. What must the island look like? Will there be anything left? How is Liam?

Monday, 9 Dec., 1300 hours

Carole—

...There are only five other adults and three kids still in the compound. They are all camping out downstairs in Faye's, the securest apartment. I will stay here and keep mopping my flooded floors to try and keep them dry and guard my books. I have not yet bagged my poetry collection and other books in my office, which I am determined will not be blown away.

God knows how the rest of the island is doing, much less battered Western Samoa. A neighbor just told me they heard on the radio that acting governor Ace Tago has declared us a disaster area. Way to go, Ace. (Acting Governor?)

12/10/91, 0030 hours

Bradpoet—

The fat lady has been screaming her fucking lungs out. This makes Ofa seem like a spring shower by comparison. I am sitting on the floor beneath my desk. No special reason, it just feels more secure. My cat is under here with me. The rest of the house, except for the nursery and the laundry room, are part of the storm. It's been eight hours since I've been past the hallway where the water is a couple of inches deep. I gather the roof above me is still on. Water seeps in around the windows. In a strange way I am happy it's night so there is just the sound, not the sights.

In a relative calm, Tom and Richard just came up to check on me. All downstairs are OK, if damp. On my last trip out of the office—three steps down the hall—I checked the barometer, which is rising for the first time in five days, almost back up onto the scale at 28 inches. Perhaps this will end someday. The house continues to shake. I put thoughts of the chaos of the next days and weeks out of my mind—the wind drives them out. We have hours of this still to go.

—12/10/91, 0900 hours—

Morning three of Val, still howling. It was a long and extremely unrestful night. Around 0400 the wind shifted to the west in screeching gusts. I was still on the floor beneath my desk—out of immediate range of exploding windows—with a hurricane lantern and a bottle of bourbon. I could tell the storm was getting to me because I was beginning to take it personally. I had the thought that this room, my office, was the only dry room left, and that the now personified wind was mounting an attack specifically upon it and me, a last hold-out.

—1400 hours—

It's calmed down enough—though still howling—for me to begin mopping up, though, with pieces of my roof missing, I'm not sure why. Something to do besides listen to roof irons flap.

What little sleep I did get last night curled beneath my desk seemed filled with technicolor dreams, with many distinct but unknown faces, magical designs in yellow and blue whose centers were never focused, and a messenger of sorts who looked like a middle-aged, grey-haired bookie or high school English teacher whose message I couldn't understand. I felt very close to my dream world.

Just back from the veranda where I managed to tug a lone pillar holding up the corner of my roof back onto slightly firmer footing. I am suddenly, numbingly tired. Could it be over after four days? I have to laugh at my attempt the other night to be philosophical about the storm qua storm. Some voice kept repeating a single word—"survivalist"—over and over in my brainstem's ear last night, rolling the word on its tongue, enjoying the separate syllables.

It's quieter; the sky is slightly brighter. The wind still whistles over all the stuff it's broken and screams now and then like a Shoshone taking scalps after a successful battle. But my dirty hair is still on my head. How many weeks will it be before I have a cold beer again?

—12/10/91, 1800 hours—

It's still hooting and whistling, but except for occasional gusts it's lost its heart. I helped Tom cut a way to his house through the fallen trees between us. Watching the roofing irons on Susan's ruined house out the window in front of my desk, the word comes to me for how they raise and lower—gills. House gills catching the wind. How they raise up and bow in homage to the god who just won them in a battle with men armed with simple nails.

It does look like a battlefield. And we handful of humans look, eat, speak and smell like survivors.

—12/10/91, 2040 hours—

After a communal dinner with our tiny clan—four adult males, two adult females, three female and one male offspring from infant to eight years old. The wind now mainly hums, sporadically flapping roof irons. The air is dry; the moon fights through the racing cloud curtain.

I need a shower and a shave and sleep. I'll get the last.

The thought strikes me that the past four days had to be shared so that they'd have meaning—be raised above simple torture—have a meaning that puts an arm around you when the walls seem about to implode. The past four days I've been writing continuous letters to you, my mom and a woman friend named Carole in San Francisco whom I never hear back from anymore. An interesting trio to replace the meaningful other—my mother, my removed poet brother and the unattainable female. There is a hazy scimitar moon in the broken limbs of the pua tree. Storms will always be shes.

Enough,
John

Dear Mom,

Bone tired, but it is a clear, calm, star-lit night with a sliver of silver moon. It calmed down enough yesterday afternoon for me to begin picking up and mopping my thoroughly trashed house—except for my office, which held, and the windowless laundry room. Funny that "calmed down enough" meant working with a gale still rushing through the house. Also I now fully realize why this operation is called "mopping up."

I slept soundly last night for the first night in four, in my office bed and not on the floor beneath my desk. Yesterday I axed a trail through the fallen trees between me and my neighbor Tom and Nancy's house. They too had lost part of their roof. My neighbor Susan's house just up the ridge may have taken a fatal blow—roof, porch, pillars gone, a flooded hulk. I watched it disintegrate within half an hour after the eye passed and the wind turned to the south. The house is only 30 yards uphill from my office window, across a short footbridge. Susan, thank god, is off-island. I watched the storm just take the house apart in about ten minutes. Gust after gust just wracked it. Old, missionary, concrete pillars that have seen a dozen hurricanes just toppled like a pile of Liam's blocks. Roofing irons tore loose and disappeared. Pieces of her porch roof, large sections, toppled toward my house and the steep cliff that separates us. (Later in the night when the wind had gotten even stronger, gusting again from the west and deflected by the ridge, it was a corner section of that porch that caused the worst structural damage to my place, taking out the corner of my veranda on that side.)

So I and my neighbors worked the rest of yesterday—till dark and a shared communal meal—starting the cleanup. There is a fine community sense to our efforts; everyone is part of this disaster tribe. The last box of defrosted chicken from my freezer went into an excellent stir-fry last night, along with defrosted veggies from other peoples' freezers. We will be eating together until the power comes back on, which could be weeks. It is much easier this way, and at dinner time—as I learned from the last storm—with no power and no electronic distractions, people will actually (can still actually!) sit around and talk, anybody's kid on anybody's lap, talk story, kid each other about little habits or neighborly quirks which before, when we were all ensconced inside our own houses, not eating together, would have been small simmering offences. (The basic unit of Samoan society—the unit of paramount importance—is what we Westerners call "the extended family," lumping the Samoan *aiga* in with all other anthropological "examples" of non-American "nuclear families." *Aiga* means in Samoan your blood-related larger family group and in-laws living within the group, but also its base meaning is "to eat." As in "eat together.")

Today was a 14-hour manual-labor day, starting at 7:30. The sun was out and the air was dry with a strange "winter" light in the sky. I hauled mattresses, carpets, pillows, cushions and mats out to dry in the sun. I opened all the remaining doors and windows and did the first, rough, cleaning pass through the devasted rooms, stacking blown-in windows and doors in piles like dead soldiers, mopping up floors that a day before had been three inches deep in storm water, sweeping out all the shredded jungle that came in through the screens. As a group, we also did several neighbors' apartments, people who are not here. But most of the day was spent trying to get Tom & Nancy's roof back on. The tribe decided that was the first priority. We got most of it done in a blazing tropical sun, all the carpentry anyway. We also got a plastic tarp over the bare roof beams of two of my neighbors'. Tomorrow we'll get jungle-salvaged roofing irons on the those roofs and maybe even get to my roof's problems. There is a certain sense of hurry-up because this morning there was another tropical storm brewing 600 miles north and headed in our general direction.

This morning we had visitors from town so we know the road is open, if treacherous and narrowed in places. The phone lines have been down since Sunday, so I've had no word from Caroline and Liam. I sent word back with the visitors from town who will try to deliver my message. I am tempted to leave and drive to town, but I am needed here and I must reclaim more of the house before bringing Liam home. The place is still very dangerous, especially for someone like Liam who thinks that every piece of splintered wood with nails sticking out of it and every downed wire is his and who would definitely want to follow me up onto the roof and use my hammer.

Not knowing how they are is hard. But I left him there for his safety and I can only hope I was right. I did hear that between five and seven Korean long-liner tuna-fishing boats were up on the reef in front of Caroline's mom's village, where they are. But her mom's house is a big, sturdy place built into the cliff face. There should have been plenty of rooms there safer than this one.I miss him so much. The last storm we went through together. For the worst nighttime hours of it he sat on my feet with his toothbrush in his hand. I miss his levity.

Sunday, 12/15/91, 1540 hours

Let's see, my last entry to you was late Wednesday night. The next three days were much the same, dawn to dusk workdays. Everything seems to take two or three times longer than you thought it would take. We had to salvage a lot of wood and roofing irons to replace the roofs, which meant fetching it out of the shredded and foot-treacherous jungle, dismantling it and piecing it back together after hauling it back. All of the houses save Susan's are reroofed well enough to take a moderate blow. I have a tarp securely fastened where my cupola used to be. Cushions and mattresses and books and pillows and floor mats took days of blistering sun to dry out.

The next storm to the north I guess went elsewhere. We've had no emergency radio broadcast since Monday when their broadcasting tower went down (we have but one AM station here). Power and phones are still out and will be for awhile, but we have water now, which is the most treasured utility.

Thursday afternoon I just dropped my hammer in the middle of a roofing job, excused myself, got in my pickup truck, and drove half the length of the island through devastation, trashed or totally destroyed villages, along roads occasionally missing their seaside lanes to check on Liam and Caroline in Leloaloa. They were safe and fine. Caroline had lost some roofing irons, which I replaced, but her house was basically unscathed. Liam was glad to see me and wanted to come home (he did want to follow me up on to Caroline's pitched roof when I fixed it), but he understood that daddy had to return home without him to—in his understanding—"fix Liam's house."

By late Saturday afternoon I finally had the place jury-rigged and cleaned enough and safe enough to go and fetch him home. He was glad to be home even though it was only half reassembled and was quick to point out all that was "broken" that daddy still had to fix—like all the downed palm trees in the yard.

Thursday, 12/19

...I have been suffering from a somewhat severe depression—the place is so trashed, everything seems pointless—but the house slowly takes on a rather bedraggled normalcy. Still no power or phone, and it will be a while longer before the repair crews get this far out.

Part of your check went for a little fake Christmas tree. Thank you. That other storm I mentioned slipped east of us and headed for the Cook Islands. I still have no doors on my oceanside verandas, and no structural repairs have been made save what limited stuff I could accomplish to make the place minimally safe and livable. Another storm would really wipe the place.

Although looting has not been much of a problem, I don't like leaving the place wide open like this, so I haven't been into my office in town very often. I will be going in this afternoon, though, so I'll end this and get it in the mail.

Love to you and all there. Have a merry Christmas and pray for me.

John

Samoa Notes 1993

Jerome Gold

I returned to Samoa in mid-June of 1993, this time not in search of a lost part of myself—I seemed to have accepted my losses or to have filled with other things the particular emptiness they left—but to visit old friends while we were all still able. Luana had died two years before. I knew this and had reconciled myself to it. I had not known that John Kneubuhl had also died. "We need to get together three or four more times," John said the last time I saw him. When we first met, six years before that time, I was in the guise of an anthropologist, he of a teacher and former screenwriter. In '89 we were more honest with ourselves: I had published my first novel and was writing almost every day; he had established himself as an islands historian and was re-emerging as a dramatist. He died of cancer in his brain a few hours before the first production of his final play.

The hurricanes of 1990 and '91 were still on everybody's mind, still dominated conversation. Chuck Brugman lost a boat in the first hurricane and another boat in the second. When Val hit, his boat was at Ofu where he had his diving operation. Friends brought it ashore and tied it up to two hardwood trees before the hurricane struck. The waves took out the trees with the boat tied to them and tumbled them up and down the reef for the next three days. Chuck was able to salvage one of the two motors. That was all.

I told him that I hadn't known there was a hurricane until I got letters from Samoa—the mainland media hadn't covered it. "Of course not," Chuck said. "Where's Samoa?"

He was at his new house in Tafuna during the storm. The road out of Tafuna was closed for four days, so he could not get to the house in Faganeanea where his daughter, Lee, lived. Lee had gone with her daughters to a friend's house in another village and sheltered there for the duration of the hurricane.

Chuck reconstructed what he thought must have happened to his house in Faganeanea: First the roof blew off. Then the windows blew out. Then the walls collapsed. Between the hurricane and the looters that came in afterward, most of his shell collection was destroyed, the looters trampling it to get at the merchandise—tapa, basketry, jewelry, shell ornaments—Lee was selling.

Diane said that Ofa—the 1990 hurricane—was a "good" hurricane. Val was "bad." Val threatened the lives of her family. Until Val, she had always assumed that Sau would be able to protect his family from anything. Sau had also assumed this. Both came to understand, because of Val, that there were things more powerful than Sau.

Diane was still angry with Val. She said if she ever met anyone named Val, she would not be able to talk to her. The psychologists came in after the hurricane and told people how they understood that they had lost their homes, etc., and they should expect to feel grief. Diane didn't think the psychologists understood that people felt anger. But what could they do about it? Smash the wind? What she wanted to do was smash their faces.

Immediately after the hurricane there was a family reunion in Hawaii. Her daughters there had assumed their family was safe because they had heard that their village was being evacuated. But, Diane pointed out to me, evacuated where? Nowhere was safe.

On the plane to Hawaii, nobody was hungry, everybody was huddled inside himself. The flight attendants did not serve dinner because no one wanted to eat. In Samoa, Diane had felt that the whole world was enduring this storm. But in Hawaii the sun was out, Christmas ornaments were up. This, too, made her angry. It was as though the hurricane in Samoa meant nothing to anyone who hadn't been through it.

The hurricane took two days to pass over the island, four miles wide at its widest part. Then they were in the eye of it. In the eye, everything was calm and peaceful,

Diane said. It was sunny. But the noise of the wind all around sounded like the roaring of a train that never arrived and never left. (Chuck also likened the noise to that of a train.) Also there was the knowledge that the eye, too, would pass over them and then they would be in for two more days of hurricane.

In her and Sau's village, houses were taken out by waves that dug so deep even their foundations disappeared. It was as though wind and sea had conspired to erase completely not only everything that recalled human life and settlement but every vestige of human memory. The waves dug so deep that they took away ancestral tombs, though the remains of some of the dead were recovered.

Later, the Red Cross came in. They wanted people to beg for food. Those who could not bring themselves to beg got nothing. The Red Cross people demanded that the government hotel get a satellite hook-up so they could watch the Superbowl game. This, when most of the population was living in Army mess tents.

The Red Cross complained that nearly twice as many Samoans claimed handouts of food as lived on the island. There are at least two ways of looking at this: 1. The Samoans, getting something for nothing, were greedy and wanted more; 2. Samoans, humiliated at being made to beg, decided to make it worth their while.

Diane told me that many Samoans, angry about the contempt shown them by Red Cross workers, decided to treat the Red Cross as a joke and competed with each other to tell off-island authorities the most outrageous lies about their losses. (According to letters I received immediately following the hurricane, Val destroyed 90% of housing in American Samoa and left 60% of the population homeless.)

There were many more applicants for FEMA grants for new houses than had houses before the hurricane. American Samoans I talked with believed that many of these applicants were Western Samoans who had been living with their sponsors. Diane remembered hearing American Samoan *matai* arguing with FEMA people about making these grants, saying that these families applying for aid were part of their own family and did not lose houses because they had none to lose, that the houses were owned by the larger family, not the smaller *aiga*. (Probably not all identified as Western Samoan were in fact Western Samoan; some likely were American Samoan who now had the opportunity to move out of their *matai*'s house into one of their own.)

Diane said that after the last hurricane everything was spackled—walls, window screens, cars, everything was spackled with small dot-like spots. At first she thought her vision had been damaged, but then she realized that what she was seeing were leaves—tiny bits of leaves that had been driven into everything that offered an exposed surface.

About Val, Sau said: "I was beaten. The problem was that after the third night I was so exhausted, I had nothing more to give. I thought we might lose the house" (and there was no place they could go to escape the hurricane if the house went, Diane had told me) "and I thought, 'Well....' There was nothing more I could do. That's why I'm building a storm shelter in the back now. If there's another hurricane like this one, I could fight for a while and then sleep in the shelter for a while and then get up and fight some more." (By "fighting," he meant bracing the frame of the house which was tearing loose from the foundation, securing the roof, reconfiguring the furniture so as to provide protection against the house itself should it collapse, etc.) "But this hurricane was stronger than me. For the first time in my life I felt defeated. I had never felt that before. I felt it was personal, between me and the hurricane, and it defeated me. I got very depressed afterward."

Changes:

1. Many more building-supplies stores now, no doubt

a response to post-Val reconstruction.

2. Did not see any cockroaches at Sau's and Diane's, though many more lizards, geckos and skinks, than I remembered seeing in '89. But there were roaches in Tafuna, I learned later when I stayed at Chuck's house. Why they should have been so plentiful in Tafuna but so scarce elsewhere on the island, I do not know.

3. Did not see anybody cut grass with a bush knife as they used to a few years ago, but there were many, many Weed-eaters.

4. Many more people, including men of working age (thirties, forties), fishing on the reef. This was rare both ten years ago and three years ago.

5. Some gangbangers from the U.S. living in Sau's and Diane's village now, either hiding out from mainland police or on a retreat from gang life. They spoke the words of respect but their demeanor was disrespectful. Saw one smoking a cigarette as he sauntered through the village.

6. Stores run by and catering to Koreans have multiplied.

7. There is a Filipino restaurant now.

8. Retail stores generally have multiplied.

9. Don't know how many people here now. Sau said over 50,000, according to the census. This would be a doubling since 1980 (according to my own sampling of population done in 1982-83, not according to 1980 census

figures which, I believe, were inflated). Regardless of how many, the island was certainly congested now. So many vehicles; the exhaust from vehicles in Pago Pago turned my stomach.

It would be difficult to chart the changes in Samoa without doing quantitative research. Yet I felt the changes, at least some of them. One response to the "feeling" of congestion in the town area: instead of going to town almost every day as I did in '82-'83 and in '89, I saved up my errands and did them all at once. Then I came back to the village as soon as I could.

A significant change in Samoa now is that the level of violence has increased. Two policemen recently were convicted of beating a prisoner to death; a man who apparently raped his stepdaughter was shot and killed by her; there have been a number of other murders in the last couple of years. Ten years ago, killing was done on impulse, almost always associated with alcohol or drug ingestion.

An exception occurred in 1983 when a Filipina engaged to be married to a Samoan was murdered by—at first nobody knew who. The murder was so brutal, so extraordinary, that no one, at least no Samoan, could believe a Samoan had done it. It must have been a *palagi*.

Or, if it was a Samoan, he must have been newly arrived from the United States. Within a week or two of the murder, the killer was caught. He was Samoan and he was, indeed, newly arrived from the United States. He had planned a robbery and it turned into something much worse.

During those ten days or two weeks before he was apprehended, not only the village in which the woman was living, but the island overall, through its news media and in everyday conversation, expressed such sorrow, such a sense of shame, that some people suggested openly that an *ifoga* be performed when the killer was caught, though it was against the law now to hold one. If I remember correctly, this view was taken by the island's most influential newspaper.

Now, in 1993, other crimes, including murder, have been calculated, and no one talks of *ifoga*. Instead, the killers and the families of the killers deny their guilt.

Almost all of these changes, or at least the rate at which they have accelerated, are owing to the hurricanes of 1990 and 1991. The increase in population is in large part due to the increase in housing which is a result of the indiscriminateness with which the FEMA grants and loans were given out. The increase in violence, expanded commercial activity and what appears to be increased unemployment are all associated with an enlarged population. An earlier hurricane (1889) was responsible for the particular brand of colonialism that was imposed on Samoa. Yet another (1966) resulted in a permanent change in the architecture of residential houses in American Samoa. The hurricane—one of Nature's great innovators, destructor and presenter of opportunity.

Here is a wonderful story. On my last evening, Chuck and I had drinks with a friend of his, Ron Palmer, whom I had not met before. Ron told this to me in Chuck's presence. When Chuck had his boat, he took Ron around to the north side of the island where he had seen a pod of dolphins earlier and towed him, outfitted in mask and snorkel, along the surface of the water. (The trick was, Chuck said, to go fast enough not to stall the engines and alarm the dolphins which are skittish of slow-moving boats, but not to go so fast as to drown the client.) This attracted the dolphins and they swam all around him, to Ron's delight. But then he noticed that one dolphin had a plastic bag hung up on its left pectoral fin and he thought "Poor thing, how terrible," and wondered how to help it. Then his attention was distracted by another dolphin and when he turned back the first one had the bag not on the left but on his right fin. Then, as Ron watched, the dolphin rolled and switched, the bag going from the right back to the left, then to the right again, and even to the dorsal. Ron said he saw another dolphin try to take the bag and the one in possession of it slapped the second one with its fin and forced it away.

Ron warned me, before telling me the story, that I would not believe it, though it's true. Hell, I believe it! I would believe it even if it weren't true!

After the Hurricane

Marilyn Stablein

On extended visits to Houston I frequently pile my books and papers into a car and drive to a friend's beach house in Galveston for the weekend. The Gulf is an hour's drive to the south.

I walk the beach at Galveston with some consistency. My path leads up and down a stretch of Pirate's Beach north to the state park and south to the horse stables. One year I walk the beach every month, another on alternating months, once after seven months. The first two times I walk this strip of Texas coastline it is the season before the hurricane, Alicia, strikes.

The hurricane so changes the beachscape, signs of the catastrophe are visible a year later. Windy turbulences buffet the coast with such force, destruction and loss are inevitable. On my beach walks after the hurricane I chart the extent of the loss and find myself making an inventory, as if somehow a detailed study might help me understand the violence and possibly avoid a future danger. The vistas of rubble, the apocalyptic aftermath, the landscapes of disaster and climates of extreme mesmerize me.

I have a sense of how dwellings stood before the hurricane, so I recognize the extent of the material loss. I am familiar with the architectural geography of beachfront property. This sense is not so much a knowledge of what kind of buildings exist but rather of where buildings once stood. Their absence is unmistakable.

In afterthought, trying to reconstruct in my mind a house that vanished, only the obvious details come to mind: a Spanish tile roof, the silhouette at sunrise, lounge chairs on a cedar deck. Unlike decay in cities, haunted houses and derelict ruins earn their woeful, frightening reputations through years of neglect or abuse. A hurricane, on the other hand, instantly changes an occupied, modern beach house with all amenities into a complete and utter ruin.

The loss assimilates into distinct stages. The greatest, to use a superlative to signify an absence or nonexistence, is total, absolute loss. For instance, once a house stood on a section of beach; now only a vacant lot remains. Remnants survive: a toaster half-buried in the sand, its cord not even frayed; a circular wrought-iron staircase leading to open sky; and a sidewalk that deadends in the sand between two palms. The remnants only hint at a former structure and contribute in no way to establish with certainty the existence of the now vanished house.

At one building site the support poles for a house stand in equidistant rows; the wooden poles emerge from the white sand like some ancient monument, an earth sculpture in a wasteland. I admire the lean visage. The foundation has integrity: through wind and rain it remains intact. But what good is a lone foundation? Where is the house? Can a foundation be true or good if it no longer supports or upholds anything?

In a list that begins with absence and grows from there, the opposite from assuming a whole and subtracting the lost parts, the second greatest loss after the vanished dwelling is the collapsed dwelling. Ruin is complete in both instances; likewise, the essence of shelter and occupancy is missing in both. The remains of the collapsed dwelling evidence structuring of some sort; only the order, the sense of cohesion and integration, is absent. Like a pile of Lincoln Logs, the pieces of a collapsed house suggest a former cohesion. A fallen house invites restructuring. The pieces are present and not missing but the boards are splintered, shattered, and irrevocably tangled. No restructuring is possible; the shards are unusable.

A partial structure characterizes a third stage of loss: an edifice remains, yet parts are missing. Some houses lack decks, chimneys or walls. The roof and front wall of one house are torn away. I wonder, Did the roof blow off in one piece and land whole somewhere? Or did the roof fall apart shingle by shingle, Spanish tile by Spanish tile?

A house without a front wall invites voyeurs. I peer into

the interior. Green drapes billow by a window; the carpeting is beige; the sofa matches the carpet. The owner's lifestyle is evident in the color and floor plan of the kitchen, the pattern of false brick paneling around the fireplace. I feel embarrassingly intimate with people I never met.

Besides the fallen and stricken buildings, there are a myriad of scattered pieces to mentally sort through. Lone objects and haphazard piles of debris signal the devastation months after the catastrophic hurricane sweeps through the neighborhood.

Earthquakes also cause structures to collapse but with a noted difference. Earthquakes are accompanied by dust: dust dislodged from ancient buildings; dust released by the impact of buildings that fall to the ground; dust freed from plaster walls. Beach rubble is not dusty. Maybe the wind disperses dust at the time of the loss of cohesion, the collapse. Maybe plaster is an anomaly in beach house construction. Sand is present but sand, unlike dirt, has distinct form and weight. Sand does not readily take flight. Even if a heavy wind stirs up the sand, the resulting sandstorm is not powdery or dusty. Sand particles manifest a cleanliness.

Beach rubble has a distinct character, unlike the ruble of demolished buildings. Demolition sites in Houston are barren, that is, the rubble consists of building materials:

wooden slats, plaster, shards, pipes and broken glass. Before the demolition, salvage workers remove doors, frames, knobs and fixtures; auctioneers cart away the furnishings. The rubble of a collapsed beach house, on the other hand, includes domestic articles: rugs, utensils, draperies, bicycles. The resulting heap is consequently large, fuller, ripe with context.

In one pile of debris, a refrigerator juts out halfway from the heap. Refrigerators do not collapse. In the rubble, a refrigerator still occupies a large, rectangular space. Even a refrigerator blown from a vanished house probably lands somewhere intact—a garage, perhaps, the bottom of a bayou, or a shopping mall parking lot. Suddenly I place great faith in the indestructibility of refrigerators. If a refrigerator takes flight, what amount of tumbling over sand, over pavement, will it take to dislodge a door, break up the metal body? Surely there must be refrigerators out there that appear, after a hurricane, more or less intact—maybe a door is missing, a side dented or a corner crushed.

I resolve to write my name and address inside my refrigerator after I drive home. I won't write it on the door; doors fall off, the hinges are not indestructible. Below my name I'll offer a reward to the finder. Like a note in a bottle set to sea or the message attached to a helium-filled balloon, in the advent of a hurricane I'll be able to chart the progress of a dislodged and errant appliance.

I circle a mound of one collapsed dwelling. The mound is not symmetrical but the center towers above the rest of the debris. Unlike the pile of leaves in my backyard where a slow, inevitable deterioration induced by mold sets in every fall, one year after Hurricane Alicia there is no rot or decay. No mold grows at the beach. Does the salt air and sand inhibit this process? There is no rust, either. The chrome dinette chair leg that sticks out of the mound still gleams.

It occurs to me that a vocabulary of ruin is sketchy, as is a vocabulary of chaos. We define objects by the order we place on them, or by their relationship to an order that surrounds them. A chair, for instance, has four legs, a seat, and a back. But how to describe a part of a chair precisely? A portion of a chair ripped apart by a hurricane? It is cumbersome to dissect the parts and name individually the parts that remain: e.g., the front leg on the right side as I face the chair is attached to one third of the seat, broken at odd angles, with the ladder back in disarray since the third rung is missing, the fourth splintered, etc.

Another thing: domestic artifacts make haunting beach debris. Since beaches are pristine by definition, any item that washes ashore, cast by water or wind, is considered debris. A ridiculous scene: a couch at high tide. Impossibly cumbersome, a couch could not have washed ashore. There are likewise no telltale signs of a prolonged ocean float, no barnacles, no seaweed bits. A couch at high tide is incongruous. A mattress, on the other hand, is more mobile. Who hasn't seen abandoned mattresses under freeways, in the woods? But a beached davenport, a drift-sofa? Impossible. A sea gull pecks stuffing from the armrest as a vulture pecks at a corpse.

I consider a floral printed bed sheet. Only an elasticized corner of the carnation-and-lily designer sheet pokes out from between two nondescript masses of debris. The bed sheet appears fresh,crisp, even though the cloth wrinkles and bunches. Like the cottons I hang out to bleach naturally in the sun, perhaps this sheet's spanking white background benefits from the prolonged exposure. How else to explain the lack of deterioration?

Another fragment invites speculation: a lone light bulb, no, two unscathed light bulbs couched in pockets of sand. Over the year, wind drove sand particles up and around the fragile glass spheres to create globe-shaped pockets of sand. The encroaching sand now cushions the bulbs. Unharmed, ironic in their persistence, their fragility, the bulbs proclaim their testimonies. No sand particles scratch the glass; the bulbs appear new. I'm tempted to take one home and screw it into a socket. If the light works, I can prove to myself some further irony: while the entire house, including the socket in which the bulb is screwed, collapsed and disintegrated, this object of light, warmth and domesticity remains unscathed.

When I focus on the ironies of mishap, the odd bits of rubble, the dislocations and chaos, I think, What if I'm caught in a hurricane? A wave of vulnerability and fear sweeps over me. If wind uproots my body, tosses and slams me against the ground, I will not survive. To confront a hurricane is sure death.

Do not worry, I assure myself. To maintain a constant fear of death is futile. The moment of death, while unpredictable as to time and place, is nevertheless inevitable. Death might come at any time. Death may be even quicker than a Texas hurricane that upheaves and howls for hours on end.

In the chaos of shock following disintegration, in the footsteps of disaster, I pick at the pieces and try to make sense of the randomness. If I count miracles like the unharmed light bulbs, the harm diminishes. That is, disaster is not complete or total if fragile light bulbs survive. To witness disorder in isolated heaps of ruin on an otherwise pristine beach is a lesson in fate and the laws of impermanence. Ultimately the external ephemera, the disorder, is outside of myself; this is both a sobering vision and a profound relief.

Glossary

aiga: Family. Extended family. Lineage. Relatives.
FEMA: Federal Emergency Management Agency.
ifoga: Ceremonial request to prevent open fighting made by representatives of the village or family of an offender to the village or family of the injured.
matai: the head of a family, extended family or lineage.
malae: Open space in the middle of a village, used as a commons, a playground, a sports field, etc.
NOAA: National Oceanic and Atmospheric Administration.
'ola:* Expression of surprise.
'ola'ola:* Expression of surprise.
palagi: Shortening of the word *papalagi*: a European or a person of European ancestry.
saimin: A thick noodle soup.

sami: Sea.
Samoa i sisifo: Western Samoa.
to'onai:* Main Sunday meal.

*An apostrophe used in a Samoan word—for example, to'onai—represents a glottal stop, so that the vowels oo, separated by an apostrophe (o'o), is pronounced as oh! oh, as though the speaker were hesitating between vowels.

Jerome Gold is the author of two novels, *The Negligence of Death* and *The Inquisitor*, and two collections of stories, *Of Great Spaces* and *Life at the End of Time*. He has published over twenty stories and essays in various journals, including Hawaii Review, Fiction Review, Left Bank and Chiron Review. A third novel, *The Prisoner's Son*, will be published by Black Heron Press.

Donna Tiapula lives in a rural village in American Samoa with her husband, Fia. She has been a teacher, a principal and a curriculum development specialist for the American Samoa Department of Education. In 1991 she received the Presidential Award for Excellence for her work in science education.

John Enright was born and raised in Buffalo, New York. He has a B.A. from the City College of New York and an M.A. in folklore from the University of California, Berkeley. After ten years as an editor and housepainter in the San Francisco Bay area, he moved to Samoa where he has resided the past dozen years, teaching, running a folk arts program and directing an environmental education organization. His short stories, poetry and essays have appeared in more than fifty books, anthologies, and periodicals. His latest book is *Ataulomа*, a collection of poetry.

Marilyn Stablein has lived in London, Kathmandu, Seattle, Houston and Berkeley. Her essays and reviews have appeared in The Sun, ZYZZYVZ, Fiction International and more than fifty other publications. Stories from her first book, *The Census Taker: Tales of a Traveler in India and Nepal*, won regional and national awards. Her other books include *Intrusions in Ice* and two collections to be published by Black Heron Press: *The ABC's of Dictionary Sex* and *Climate of Extremes.*